Country Kitchen Collection

The Dairy

William Shayer (1788-1879) *Milking Time*

Country Kitchen Collection
The Dairy

Anna Nicholas

Tom R.W.S. Lloyd (1849-1910) *Milk for the Calves*

Grange
BOOKS

ACKNOWLEDGEMENTS
All pictures by courtesy of The Bridgeman Art Library

Returning Home by W. Mackenzie (19th century) Walker Galleries, Harrogate/Bridgeman Art Library, London.
A Farmyard in Normandy by Claude Monet (1840-1926) Louvre, Paris/Bridgeman Art Library, London/Lauros-Giraudon. The Small Collation, also Called the Carafe of Orgeat by Henri Roland de la Porte (1724-1793) Louvre, Paris/Bridgeman Art Library, London./Giraudon. Still Life by Alexander van Adriaenssen (1587-1661) Prado, Madrid/Bridgeman Art Library, London. Dutch Dairy Farmers, 1829-30 (engraving) by L. Springer (d.1871) British Library/Bridgeman Art Library, London. Still Life of Fruits, Cheese and Bread by Sebastian Stoskopff (1596/99-1657) Musée des Beaux-Arts, Le Havre/Bridgeman Art Library, London/Giraudon. Afternoon Tea by Isidor Verheyden (1846-1905) Private Collection/Bridgeman Art Library, London. The Chocolate Pot by Jean-Etienne Liotard (1702-1789) Gemaldgalerie, Dresden/Bridgeman Art Library, London. Déjeuner sur l'Herbe by Édouard Manet (1832-1883) Musée d'Orsay, Paris/Bridgeman Art Library, London. Tea Time by Jacques Jourdan (1880-1916) Gavin Graham Gallery, London/Bridgeman Art Library, London. The Milkmaid by Adrianus Johannes Groenewegen (1874-1963) Private Collection/Bridgeman Art Library, London. Feeding the Chickens by David Woodlock (1842-1929) Waterman Fine Art Ltd., London/Bridgeman Art Library, London. The Dairy Door, Farringford, Lord Tennyson's Home by Helen Allingham (1848-1926) Christopher Wood Gallery, London/Bridgeman Art Library, London. The Milkmaid by William Shayer Snr. (1788-1879) Cheltenham Art Gallery & Museums, Gloucestershire/Bridgeman Art Library, London. Still Life by Angel Planells i Cruanyes (b.1901) Collection of J. B. Cendros, Barcelona/Bridgeman Art Library, London. Still Life with Cheese by Guillaume Romain Fouace (1827-1895) Musée des Beaux-Arts, Le Havre/Bridgeman Art Library, London. Milking in the Fields by Samuel Palmer (1805-1881) Bury Art Gallery & Museum, Lancs./Bridgeman Art Library, London. Still Life with Brioche by Édouard Manet (1832-1883) Christie's, London/Bridgeman Art Library, London. Breakfast at Berneval, 1898 by Pierre Auguste Renoir (1841-1919) Private Collection/Bridgeman Art Library, London. Uninvited Guests by Edgar Hunt (1876-1953) Eaton Gallery, London/Bridgeman Art Library, London. Still Life with a Beaker, Cheese, Butter and Biscuits by Floris van Schooten (fl.1605-1655) Harold Samuel Collection/Bridgeman Art Library, London. The White Table Cloth by John Shirley-Fox (1860-1939) Private Collection/Bridgeman Art Library, London. The Lunch by Pierre Auguste Renoir (1841-1919) Staedel Institute, Frankfurt/Bridgeman Art Library, London. The Picnic by James Jacques Joseph Tissot (1836-1902) Tate Gallery, London/Bridgeman Art Library, London. Animals in a Pond by Eugène Boudin (1824-1898) Musée des Beaux-Arts, Le Havre/Bridgeman Art Library, London. Milking Time by William Shayer Snr. (1788-1879) York City Art Gallery/Bridgeman Art Library, London. Milk for the Calves by Thomas James R.W.S. Lloyd (1849-1910) Towner Art Gallery, Eastbourne/Bridgeman Art Library, London. Girl with Two Calves by Walter Hunt (1861-1941) Wolverhampton Art Gallery/Bridgeman Art Library, London. Still Life with Eggs by Isadore Edmond Henri Opsomer (1878-1967) Musée National d'Art Modeme, Paris/ Bridgeman Art Library, London. Glass of Milk by Stanley Cursiter (1887-1976) City of Edinburgh Museums & Art Galleries/Bridgeman Art Library, London. An Old Woman Cooking Eggs, 1618 by Diego Rodriguez de Silva y Velasquez (1599-1660) National Gallery of Scotland, Edinburgh/Bridgeman Art Library, London. Feeding Time by Edgar Hunt, 1928 (1876-1955) Bonhams, London/Bridgeman Art Library, London. A Devonshire Farmyard by Walter Hunt (1861-1941) Bonhams, London/Bridgeman Art Library

The Publishers have made every effort to trace the copyright holders of material reproduced within this compilation. If, however, they have inadvertantly made any error they would be grateful for notification.

Published in 1996
by Grange Books
An imprint of Grange Books Plc.
The Grange
Grange Yard
London SE1 3AG

ISBN 1 85627 744 5

This book is not intended to be an in-depth look at the technique of cooking: there are a myriad of books which do just this and which go into the nuances of producing many of the dishes described in this volume, most of which have been around for a very long time and exist in many variations even across national boundaries. It is a celebration of food in its wider sense; as an important part of the development of civilized behaviour in which society is bonded together in the acts of eating, discussing and depicting food which is, after all, a prime necessity for our continued existence.

A man has no better thing under the sun
than to eat, and drink, and be merry.

Ecclesiastes 8, 15

Walter Hunt (1861-1941) Girl with Two Calves

Foreword

As the title implies, these are long-established recipes and some of the dishes have very ancient origins indeed. Many developed when little thought was given to the dangers of cholesterol and the perils of too much fat in the diet. The products of the dairy farm were simply seen as part of the bounty of nature, there for all to eat and enjoy. Today we are more cautious, perhaps to a ludicrous degree when some of us are feeding our infants and young children low fat versions of foods that are vital to the growth of healthy bones and teeth and the sound development of their growing bodies. Milk and cheese are equally important where older people are concerned to help guard against the dangers of brittle bone disease.

The debate as to the healthiness of butter versus modern vegetable spreads has still not been fully resolved though most would agree that butter tastes superior and has very much better qualities when used in cooking. The answer has always been that moderation lies in all things and that over-reliance on one food or group of foods is hardly sensible if we wish to achieve a lifetime of good health.

If we concentrate on a balanced diet, taking foods from many different groups, such as fresh fruit and vegetables, pulses and cereals, meats and fish, we need hardly deny ourself once in a while for a special occasion meal, perhaps, one or two of the delicious recipes in this book which we can eat with the clear conscience that they are a good source of protein, calcium and many other vital nutriments, too.

Apart from the health and nutrition aspect, do not forget the extreme versatility of milk and its many by-products. Where would we be without eggs, cream, cheese and yogurt? Indeed, the food traditions of the Western world would immediately collapse or would at least be infinitely poorer if they were to suddenly disappear from the face of the earth. Last but not least, we must face the indisputable fact that everything produced from dairy and farmyard is uniquely delicious.

Eggs Benedict

The original version of this dish was probably poached eggs served on a bed of creamed salt cod (brandade de morue).

Many people swear by the addition of a little vinegar to the water when poaching eggs. This may not be strictly necessary although it possibly helps the eggs to coagulate. What is of paramount importance is that the eggs are as fresh as possible when no trouble should arise if they are slipped from their shells and slid into $1\frac{1}{2}$ inches or so of barely simmering water and cooked as gently as possible for about 3 minutes. Do not attempt to cook more than two eggs at a time. Served on toast or a croûton and covered in a good Hollandaise sauce they become *Eggs Benedict*, the basis of many a hearty American breakfast.

No man can be wise on an empty stomach.

George Eliot (1819-1880)

Isidore Edmond Henri Opsomer (1878-1967) *Still Life with Eggs*

7

Blancmange

This is an ancient dish with its roots in medieval times when it was originally a savoury dish containing white meats, such as chicken, bound together with almond milk. Guaranteed to bring back childhood memories, when it may have been served a little too frequently, this nursery dessert has been almost forgotten. However, it is still as nourishing as it always was and is a good way of getting milk into today's children.

Blend 4 level tablespoons of cornflour (cornstarch) into a smooth paste with 2 tablespoons taken from 1pint (2½ cups) of milk. Boil the remaining milk with a piece of lemon rind and strain onto the blended mixture, stirring well. Return to the pan, bring back to the boil and cook for a further 3 minutes until the mixture has thickened. Pour into a dampened jelly mould and allow to set. Other flavourings can also be used, such as melted chocolate, coffee essence etc., but plain blancmange is also good served with soft fruits.

Junket

Here is another echo from the past. The enzyme rennet, also used in cheesemaking, is intrinsic to this dish and ordinary pasteurized milk must be used to avoid killing this living substance. There are commercial products containing rennet which also provide flavouring and colour but here we are using ordinary liquid rennet.

Gently heat 1 pint (2½ cups) of milk until just warm. Remove from the heat and stir in 1 level tablespoon of sugar until dissolved. Then stir in 1 teaspoon of rennet. Pour into a serving dish and leave undisturbed in a warm place for a good hour or so until set. Sprinkle with freshly grated nutmeg and chill well before serving.

What is patriotism but the love of good things we ate in our childhood?

Lin Yutang

Stanley Cursiter (1887–1976) *Glass of Milk*

Isidor Verheyden (1846–1905) *Afternoon Tea*

10

Cat's Tongues

These feather-light little biscuits originate from France where they are known as *langues de chat*. They are often served with desserts and ice creams or a glass of Madeira wine. This quantity makes 50-60 as it is not worth making fewer. Work 4½ oz (½ generous cup) soft unsalted butter and 4½ oz (1 generous cup) castor sugar together until smooth and creamy. Add three unbeaten egg whites, one at a time, stirring well after each addition. Gradually incorporate 4½ oz (1 cup) sifted flour and 1½ teaspoons of real vanilla essence. Using a pastry or icing tube fitted with a plain nozzle, force 3-inch strips of the mixture onto a buttered baking tray leaving spaces in between for them to rise. Bake for 6-8 minutes in a pre-heated hot oven. For an attractive finish, lightly dust the biscuits with castor sugar before putting them in the oven.

'Stand the Church clock at ten to three? And is there honey still for tea?'

Rupert Brooke (1887-1915)

Devonshire Splits

Afternoon tea-parties have to a large extent gone out of fashion but there are signs of revival, especially in some of the larger, prestigious hotels. Along with wafer-thin cucumber sandwiches and Victoria Sponge Cake, scones are a must, served split and filled with thick clotted cream and strawberry or raspberry preserve.

Sieve 8 oz (2 cups) self raising flour into a bowl with 1 tablespoon of sugar and a pinch of salt. Incorporate a lightly beaten egg and 5 tablespoons of sour milk and lightly mix to a soft dough. Turn out onto a floured board, roll out to a thickness of about ½ an inch and cut into 2-inch rounds with a fluted pastry cutter. Place on a greased baking tray and cook in a hot oven for about 15 minutes.

Jean-Etienne Liotard (1702-1789) *The Chocolate Pot*

Chocolate Mousse

Heat a 4-oz (110 g) slab of dark bitter chocolate in a *bain-marie* or double saucepan. When the chocolate has melted, add 6 oz (1 scant cup) castor sugar, 2 tablespoons of water and stir until the sugar has dissolved. Add five egg yolks, one at a time, beating all the while. Remove the saucepan from the heat and stir in a small liqueur glass of cognac, Cointreau or Grand Marnier. Beat the whites of the five eggs until stiff, then carefully fold into the chocolate mixture. Pour into individual glasses and refrigerate for at least 2 hours before serving. Serve with *langues de chat* or ratafia biscuits.

The proof of the pudding is in the eating.

Proverb

Édouard Manet (1832-1883) *Déjeuner sur l'herbe (The Picnic)*

Quiche Lorraine

This speciality of Northern France is now popular everywhere and has inspired many variations. It makes an excellent lunch dish served with a mixed salad and is good to take on a picnic where it is suitably hearty for healthy appetites. The following is very nearly authentic but if you do not eat meat you could substitute grated cheese or a little sautéed onion or leek as a filling.

Make some shortcrust pastry with 4 oz (1 cup) of plain flour, 1 tablespoon each of butter and lard or dripping, a pinch of salt and enough cold water to bind the ingredients so that they form a soft dough. Roll into a ball and leave to rest in a cool place for 1 hour. Line a buttered flan or pie dish with the pastry and cover the base with 6 rashers (slices) of bacon which have been previously diced and fried for a few minutes. Beat 2 eggs into $^1/_2$ pint ($1^1/_2$ cups) cream, add salt and pepper and pour over the bacon. Bake in a hot oven for about 30 minutes. Allow to cool slightly before serving.

Strawberries and Cream

The two ladies in the picture opposite look as though a good bowl of strawberries and cream would not go amiss. This is the classic summertime treat, eagerly anticipated in earlier times because of the fruit's short season. Nowadays, with the benefits of modern transport, strawberries seem to be available all the year round: but they are still best eaten in a quiet, beautiful garden on a hot, lazy summer's day.

Avoid washing the fruit if at all possible. If you must, wash it before you remove the stalks, to avoid water getting inside the fruit and making it soggy. Drain well, sprinkle with a little castor sugar and allow to macerate for a short time. Serve with thick clotted cream. If you are watching calories, do as the Italians and serve the strawberries with sugar and lemon juice or *au naturel* with a surprising sprinkling of ground black pepper.

Strawberry Shortcake

Another way of serving strawberries which has become a classic in its own right.

Rub 4 oz (¹/₂ cup) of butter into 1 lb (4 cups) self raising flour until it resembles fine breadcrumbs. Add 2 tablespoons of sugar and mix to a stiff dough with a cup of milk. Divide the mixture between two buttered tins and bake in a very hot oven for about 20 minutes. When cool, sandwich the two together with a thick layer of sweetened whipped cream in which halved strawberries have been embedded. Decorate the top with more whipped cream with strawberries crushed into it.

Jacques Jourdan (1880–1916) *Tea Time*

Rice Pudding

This is an Austrian version of the traditional rice pudding and introduces a higher level of sophistication to this humble dish elevating it from nursery to dinner party status.

Boil 12 oz (1¹⁄₂ cups) white rice in 2 pints (5 cups) milk until tender. Strain. Put 2 tablespoons of butter, 4 oz (¹⁄₂ cup) sugar, 1 tablespoon each of orange and lemon juice into a heavy pan and cook together. Add this mixture to the rice, mix well and allow to cool. Stir in 4 teaspoons of rum and put a layer of the mixture in the bottom of a buttered baking dish. Over this spread a layer of strawberry jam or jelly and a layer of apple sauce. Repeat the layers of rice and jam and apple sauce until the dish is almost full. Beat up 3 egg whites with 2 tablespoons of castor sugar and a drop of vanilla essence and spread over the top of the pudding. Bake in a hot oven for 15 minutes and serve immediately.

The discovery of a new dish does more for human pleasure than the discovery of a new star.

Jean Anthelme Brillat-Savarin (1755-1826)

Adrianus Johannes Groenewegen (1874-1963) *The Mill*

16

Spaghetti alla Carbonara

You could cook this dish in half the time it would take to order a takeout meal and you are guaranteed to find it twice as delicious and half as expensive. This quantity serves 4.

Put ³/₄ lb (340 g) of spaghetti on to cook. Drain well, place in a heated bowl and keep warm. Meanwhile, gently cook a cupful of finely diced bacon or *pancetta* in a little butter until lightly browned. Add the bacon and a little of the cooking fat to the spaghetti, gently stir and keep warm. Break 5 eggs into a bowl and beat them up with a good bit of chopped parsley and some black pepper. Stir into the spaghetti/bacon mix when you will find that their heat will cook the egg slightly. Serve as quickly and as hot as possible with generous amounts of Parmesan cheese.

Alexander van Adriaenssen (1587-1661) *Still Life*

18

David Woodlock (1842-1929) *Feeding the Chickens*

A Perfect Omelette

As everyone knows, there is only one infallible method – your own. This is often a reasonable enough assumption for there are a multitude of ways whereby an acceptable result can be achieved and this does not only apply to omelettes. Although rustling up an omelette for supper is regarded as a simple matter, to produce a perfect one needs a little more care. The same goes for all the other ways of cooking eggs. Here are a few thoughts on the subject:

1 Avoid beating the eggs too hard. Stirring them around a bit with a fork is preferable.
2 It goes without saying that the eggs should be as fresh as possible.
3 Do not attempt to make a very large omelette – it is better to make several smaller ones of 2-3 eggs.
4 Remember that eggs are the star of this dish – do not allow your choice of filling to overpower them.
5 Warm your pan beforehand and melt a good knob of butter until it is sizzling and light brown in colour.
6 Tilt and fold the egg mixture as you go, allowing the uncooked portions to come in contact with the hot pan. Do all this as quickly as possible stopping when the surface still looks slightly uncooked. This will ensure that the omelette is delicate and tender rather than tough and unappetizing.

19

Diego Rodriguez de Silva y Velasquez (1599-1660) *Old Woman Cooking Eggs*

Egg Soup

Although made from everyday ingredients this soup is satisfying and nourishing and has an exotic air about it. It is known as Oeufs Noyés in France.

Chop up 4 small onions and the white parts of 4 leeks and put them in 2½ pints (6 cups) of cold water. Add 1 or more crushed cloves of garlic, a pinch of fennel and thyme, salt and pepper and cook for 20 minutes. Put in a tablespoon of olive oil and a pinch of saffron and boil for another 5 minutes. Carefully break 1 egg per person and let them gently poach in the liquid. Remove when done and keep warm. Fry pieces of bread in olive oil, put a piece in each deep, warm soup plate, place an egg on each and pour over the soup.

Avgolemono

This could be regarded as one of the Greek national dishes and possibly has very ancient origins indeed. It is a delicate soup where the flavour of the main ingredient is of tantamount importance. Don't even bother to make it unless you are prepared to make fresh chicken stock from scratch.

Bring 3 pints (7½ cups) good chicken broth to the boil. Add 3 oz (½ cup) Italian *arborio* rice and cook until just tender. Season with salt to taste. Beat 2 egg yolks and the juice of a lemon together in a very large bowl and gradually whisk the broth and rice into it. Return to the pan and heat very gently until the soup thickens slightly. On no account let the mixture boil. Can be served with a sprinkling of cinnamon.

Don't teach your grandmother to suck eggs.

Proverb

Crème Brûlée

This dessert originated in England: it was invented at Trinity College, Cambridge where it was known as Trinity Cream or Burnt Cream and they still make it the same way but without sweetening the cream. It is a good idea to make this dish the day before you need it so that the custard can be well chilled and firm before you embark on the final stages.

Slowly heat 1 pint (2 cups) of double (heavy) cream and a bruised vanilla pod until it reaches boiling point but no further. Meanwhile, beat up 6 egg yolks with 2 tablespoons of castor sugar. Slowly add the hot cream, beating all the while, then heat the mixture in a double saucepan, or a bowl over a saucepan of hot water, and stir until almost boiling when the mixture should thickly coat the back of a spoon. Pour into a gratin dish or individual ramekins and chill well. When the cream is cold and set, sprinkle it with a $\frac{1}{4}$-inch layer of castor sugar and place under a very hot grill. Remove when the sugar has caramelized and has produced an attractive gold and dark brown mottled effect, rather like tortoiseshell.

22

Helen Allingham (1848-1926) *The Dairy Door, Farringford*, Lord Tennyson's Home

Milk Shakes

There is really nothing like a glass of ice-cold milk as a delicious thirst-quencher or as the base of a light, nutritious meal, especially for children and members of the older generation who particularly need plenty of calcium in their diet. However, children have an uncanny knack of developing an aversion to things which 'do them good': what better way to overcome this problem than to serve this valuable food in the form of delicious milk shakes.

Try whizzing up a banana or other soft fruits such as strawberries and raspberries with a little sugar or use other flavourings such as drinking chocolate, coffee essence or even chopped nuts added to cold milk in the food processor or liquidizer. You could mix in fruit yogurt and add a scoop of ice cream before serving for a touch of instant appeal.

Henri Roland de la Porte (1724-1793) *The Small Collation*

*Plain cooking cannot be
entrusted to plain cooks.*

Countess Morphy

Claude Monet (1840-1926) *A Farmyard in Normandy*

Moules à la Marinière

Butter and cream and cider are an intrinsic part of the cuisine of Normandy. Indeed any dish cooked à la Normande will certainly contain some or all of these vital ingredients. Married to succulent seafood, which is locally available in such freshness and abundance, you have an irresistible partnership.

Scrub, scrape and de-beard about 6 lb (3 kg) mussels, discarding any which are already open. Simmer together 1 cup of dry white wine or cider with a small chopped onion or a couple of shallots and a few sprigs of parsley for about 5 minutes. Cook the mussels in batches in this liquid until they open. Discard any which fail to open; this indicates that they were already dead. Strain the poaching liquid and gradually whisk in a cup of cream and a knob of unsalted butter. Add some chopped chives or parsley and pour over the mussels. Eat with plenty of bread to mop up the juices and some wine or cider to drink, whatever you used to cook the mussels.

Here is another good way to serve mussels. Arrange cooked mussels in their half shells in a flat ovenproof dish. Make a stuffing from white breadcrumbs, a little garlic and plenty of chopped parsley bound together with melted butter. Cover the mussels with the mixture and press it well down. Cook very briefly under a hot grill and serve immediately.

Sebastian Stoskopff (1596/99–1657) *Still Life of Fruits, Cheese and Bread*

Fondue

In Switzerland the cheese is prepared in a special fireproof earthenware dish called a caquelon. A long fondue fork is also supplied to each person. In the absence of the genuine article, you could use an enamel casserole or other suitable container.

Rub the inside of the cooking pot with a cut clove of garlic. Add 1 pint (2 cups) dry white wine and, as it is heating, gradually stir in 3 cups of grated Gruyère cheese. As bubbles begin to break the surface, add 2 teaspoons of cornflour (cornstarch) blended with 4 tablespoons of kirsch and a little pepper and freshly grated nutmeg. Serve in the pot in which the fondue has been cooked and keep it slightly bubbling by placing it on the table over a small spirit stove. The idea is to dip cubes of French bread into the mixture twirling them about a bit before eating them. The custom is that anyone losing a piece of bread in the fondue must treat the assembled company to a bottle of wine. Fonduta, the Italian version, is made with Fontina cheese.

Welsh Rarebit

In times past, when meals seemed to have had very many more courses, this would have been served as a savoury to round off an already generous dinner. Nowadays, this would go down quite nicely as an occasional snack.

Melt 2 tablespoons of butter over a very low heat, or ideally over hot water in a double saucepan, and add 2 cups of grated matured farmhouse Cheddar cheese. Gradually add a cup of beer, stirring till smooth. Then add a teaspoon of made mustard, a little *paprika* and 2 beaten egg yolks. Gently cook, stirring all the while, until the mixture thickens. Serve on slices of hot toast – you could brown the rarebits under a hot grill if you like.

St. Nicholas Day Letters

On 5 December, the feast of St. Nicholas, little children in Holland leave their shoes by the fireplace to be filled with presents. Among the gifts can probably be found the boter letters, pastries formed into the initial letter of their names.

Use either home-made or bought frozen flaky pastry, roll thinly and cut into strips 3 inches long and 2 inches wide. Mix together 6 oz (1½ cups) ground almonds, 2 eggs, 3 oz (scant ½ cup) castor sugar and 3 oz (scant cup) icing or confectioner's sugar, a few drops of almond essence and the juice of half a lemon. Mix to a smooth paste, roll into small individual sausage shapes and wrap the pastry strips around each shape. Seal with beaten eggs and bend into the required initials. Bake in a hot oven for 30 minutes or so and leave to cool.

Gingerbread

This is another sweetmeat linked to an occasion, in this case Guy Fawkes Night, when it is served along with sausages and potatoes cooked in the embers of the bonfire to an accompaniment of fireworks such as sparklers and Catherine wheels.

Boil together half a cup of brown sugar with 1 lb (450 g) black treacle until the sugar has dissolved. Remove from the heat and stir in 4 oz (½ cup) of butter. Sift 1 lb (4 cups) of self raising flour into a bowl and add 2 good teaspoons of ground ginger and 1 teaspoon of ground cinnamon. Put 1 teaspoon of bicarbonate of soda (baking soda) into the hot mixture and when it froths add in the dry ingredients and mix to a soft dough. Leave to rest overnight. Next day, spread the mixture out on a baking tray to a depth of about 1½ inches. Brush the surface well with beaten egg mixed with milk, decorate with whole almonds and bake in a moderate oven for about an hour. Cut into squares when cool.

L. Springer (d.1871) *Dutch Dairy Farmers*, 1829-1830 (engraving)

Lemon Cheesecake

This dish can be prepared well in advance which is useful when you wish to get the dessert course out of the way while you concentrate on the others. It is also extremely simple to make as it involves no cooking whatsoever.

Melt two tablespoons of butter in a thick saucepan and add to it about 4 oz (a generous cup) of crushed whole wheat cookies or digestive biscuits. Stir until well mixed with the butter, then line the base of a lightly oiled flan tin by pressing the crumbs evenly over it. Leave to harden in the refrigerator. Meanwhile, beat together $1^{1/2}$ lb (3 cups) cream cheese with the squeezed juice of 2 lemons and the grated rind of one of them, plus 2 tablespoons of castor sugar. When thoroughly blended, pour the mixture onto the biscuit crumb base in the tin, cover with plastic wrap and chill thoroughly. Decorate as you like, just before serving. Fresh strawberries or other soft fruit would be very nice indeed.

Grub first, then ethics.
Berthold Brecht

William Shayer, Senior (1788-1879) *The Milkmaid*

30

Oeufs sur le Plat

As the name implies, these are fried eggs served in the dish in which they have been cooked — a good way of getting your eggs piping hot and the yolks intact. Use shallow metal dishes or earthenware or other fireproof containers.

Put melted butter in the dish and gently slide in the eggs, usually 2 per person. If you cover the dish there will be no need to baste the eggs in order to set the yolks. Cook either gently on top of the stove or in a moderate oven for a few minutes until the whites are set. Remember to make allowances for the fact that eggs in metal or enamel dishes will go on cooking even when removed from the heat source. In any case, you should be able to avoid tough, 'lacy' whites.

Angel Planells I Cruanyes (b.1901) *Still Life*, c.1925

Never put all your eggs in one basket.

Proverb

Green Salad with Roquefort and Walnuts

Roquefort is the king of cheeses and its price sadly reflects this fact. Nevertheless, it is so delicious and the flavour is so intense that a little can go a long way, in salad dressings, for instance. Try a few teaspoons crumbled and mixed into an ordinary vinaigrette when it will be uplifted beyond belief. Or mash a little with some brandy and a little thin cream to dress an ordinary green salad.

Blend together in a bowl 2 tablespoons wine vinegar, 1 tablespoon Dijon mustard, 4 tablespoons olive oil, 2 tablespoons cream and salt and pepper. Assemble a mixture of crisp salad greens such as frisée or curly endive, firm lettuce and chicory and coat with the dressing, adding some chopped parsley or chives, a generous amount of diced Roquefort and some walnut halves. For a more robust meal, slices of ham or *prociutto* can be added. Slices of Gruyère can be substituted for the Roquefort for a milder flavour.

Gnocchi

These are delicious little dumplings made from cheese and semolina flour and baked with butter or a sauce in the oven. Another version can be made by substituting mashed potatoes and flour for the semolina.
Like pasta, they are rather fiddly to make. Unless you are dedicated to the idea of making your own, you will find that the ready-made article can be quite easily obtained from your local supermarket or delicatessen.

Lay the gnocchi in overlapping rows in a well buttered gratin dish. Dot with plenty of butter and grated Parmesan cheese and bake until nicely browned. You could serve a light tomato sauce as an accompaniment although a mixed salad would go just as well.

Guillaume Romain Fouace (1827–1895) *Still Life with Cheese*

Samuel Palmer (1805–1881) *Milking in the Fields*

34

Syllabub

This is an old English drink originally made from warm milk straight from the cow. This is the more modern dessert version.

Finely grate the rind of 2 lemons, avoiding the pith, and add it to the juice of one of the lemons, 3 tablespoons of castor sugar and a glass of sherry. Leave to marinate overnight. Next day, put the mixture in a large bowl and whip in 1 pint (2 cups) double (heavy) cream until it stands up in soft peaks. Serve well chilled in pretty glasses.

This is similar to the Italian *Zabaglione* in which *Marsala*, the sweet wine of Sicily is used instead of sherry. For a less rich version half cream and half milk could be used but you would need to fold in a couple of stiffly beated egg whites at the last minute.

Édouard Manet (1832-1883) *Still Life with Brioche*

Brioche

Brioche is richer and lighter than ordinary bread as it contains milk, eggs and butter. It comes in the form of small breakfast rolls or in large loaves which are cut up and eaten with butter and jam. Sometimes the brioche is hollowed out and stuffed with meat pâté or mushrooms cooked in cream.

The Italian panettone is of similar texture and is delicious cut into thick slices, toasted and covered with a mixture of soft summer fruits and briefly placed to toast under a hot grill.

Mix together 1 oz yeast (1 cake compressed yeast), 4 oz (1 cup) flour and 2 tablespoons warm water until the dough forms a ball. Put it in a warm place until it has doubled its size. Meanwhile, break 3 eggs into 12 oz (3 cups) flour. Beat well, adding a little more water if the mixture appears too dry. Add 4 oz ($^1/_2$ cup) melted butter, a pinch of salt and a tablespoon of sugar. Mix well with your hands for 5 minutes. Take the yeast and flour mixture and add it to this making sure the two are well amalgamated. Cover and allow to stand for 6 hours or so until twice its original size. Knead carefully and leave in a cool place overnight. Next day, place the dough in a tin or buttered *savarin* mould. Rest for half an hour or so, then bake in a very hot oven for 35 minutes, covering the top with foil to prevent burning.

Pierre Auguste Renoir (1841-1919) *Breakfast at Berneval*

Muesli

This traditional Swiss breakfast dish has come into its own again now that a high-fibre diet is generally recommended. Many versions can be bought ready-made but they are often too sweet and contain too high a proportion of oats. It is an easy matter to make muesli for yourself and you can then please yourself as to the varieties and proportions of the ingredients you put in it.

Soak a good cupful of rolled oats overnight in 6 tablespoons (a good ¹/₂ cup) of water or fresh orange or apple juice. Next day, wash and grate 4 sweet apples, skins and all, into the oats. Add the juice of a lemon, half a cup of shelled walnuts, 2 tablespoons of bran, some raisins and sultanas and a little brown sugar. Serve with sliced bananas, or whatever other fresh fruit or berries are in season, with a little cold milk to taste. This is probably all you need to start the day and is guaranteed to keep you going till lunchtime.

Chicken Fricassée

Many people are cutting down on red meats these days without converting entirely to a vegetarian diet. For them, lower fat white meats and fish are still an option. This dish is a little on the rich side but delicious for all that — perhaps to be enjoyed once in a while. At all costs try to obtain a free-range chicken, a bird which has roamed about in the open, pecking about for a variety of foods and enjoying its life. It will, in any case, taste all the better for this.

Joint the chicken and cook it gently in a deep pan or casserole in a little butter without allowing it to brown. Sprinkle in 2 tablespoons of flour, stir around and cook for a few minutes. Add enough boiling water to cover the chicken, stirring well as you go. Add an onion studded with cloves and some parsley stalks tied in a bundle. Bring back to the boil and simmer till the chicken is tender. Mix up the yolks of 2 eggs with half a cup of cream and a little of the stock from the saucepan. Fold the mixture into the stock with the chicken which will result in an excellent thickened sauce.

Fish Pie

This is a delicious family dish, usually made from cod, whiting, haddock, or whatever white fish is available. For an added punch, a little smoked haddock could be mixed in with the other fish.

From a selection of cooked white and smoked fish, remove all skin and bone and break it up into large flakes. Meanwhile, hard boil a few eggs and cut them into quarters. Boil some potatoes and mash them with a little butter, milk, salt and pepper. Make a well seasoned white sauce and stir in a good handful of chopped parsley. Put the fish into an ovenproof dish with a few cooked prawns, if liked, a few capers, the hard-boiled eggs and the sauce. Make sure the ingredients are evenly dispersed throughout the dish but be careful not to break up the fish flakes and eggs too much. Cover the top with a layer of mashed potatoes and a little grated cheese and brown in a hot oven until thoroughly heated through.

Edgar Hunt (1876-1953) *Uninvited Guests*

Sole Meunière

This fish has such a fine taste and texture that it would be criminal to cook it with any but the simplest of ingredients. The miller's wife obviously discovered long ago that all that was required was a freshly caught sole, some good country butter and a sprig or two of chopped parsley from her garden. If you have the time and inclination to clarify the butter in which you are going to cook the fish, so much the better. Trim and clean (or have it done for you by your fishmonger) 1 medium sole per person.

Wash and thoroughly dry the fish and coat it lightly in flour. Heat a good knob of butter in a skillet or frying pan and fry the fish for 5 or 6 minutes on each side, according to their thickness. Season well with salt and pepper as you go. Put the fish onto a hot serving dish and pour the hot cooking butter over. Sprinkle with chopped parsley and serve immediately.

In another dish from France, known as *Sole Bonne Femme*, the fish is cooked in a rich sauce of shallots and mushrooms made with white wine and thickened with egg yolks.

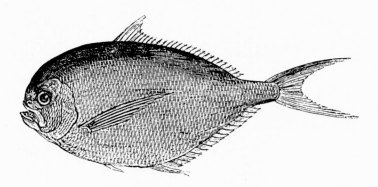

40

Gougère

Most of the traditional dishes of the Burgundy region of France – Coq au Vin, Escargots Bourguinonne, Jambon Persillé de Bourgogne – have been developed to complement the marvellous wines of the area. Some even include local wines in their list of ingredients and all are redolent of the vineyards and countryside from which they have sprung. Gougère is such a dish and is robust enough to be drunk with a full-bodied Burgundy.

For this recipe you will need 6 eggs, 6¼ oz (1½ cups) grated Gruyère cheese, 4 oz (½ cup) butter, 8 oz (2 cups) flour and ¾ pint (2 cups) of milk. Put the butter in a thick saucepan with a pinch of salt. Pour on half the milk, stirring constantly. Make a smooth paste with the flour and the rest of the milk and pour the boiling milk onto it, still stirring. Return to the saucepan and break the eggs into the milk, one at a time, and then add the Gruyère. The mixture will become thick and creamy. Put into a deep buttered pie dish, sprinkling a little more cheese on top. Bake for half an hour in a hot oven. Good eaten either hot or cold.

Hitchcock watched with fascination as his wife made a cheese soufflé. His eyes remained glued to the oven door as it was cooking. 'What on earth is going on behind that door?' he asked every few minutes. By the time the soufflé was ready to be taken out of the oven, Hitchcock was a nervous wreck. 'No more soufflés until we get a new oven with a glass door. I can't stand the suspense!'

Sir Alfred Hitchcock (1889-1980)

Floris van Schooten (fl. c.1612) *Still Life with Beaker, Cheese, Butter and Biscuits*

Victoria Sandwich Cake

All that seems to be missing from the scene opposite is a feather-light sponge cake sandwiched together with a home-made preserve, raspberry, perhaps. This cake was named after Queen Victoria and is not at all difficult to make.

You will need 6 oz ($^3/_4$ cup) butter, 6 oz ($^3/_4$ cup) castor sugar, 6 oz ($1^1/_2$ cups) self-raising flour, 3 eggs, beaten, and some fruit preserve. Butter two sandwich cake tins and line the bases with baking parchment or greaseproof paper. Beat the butter and sugar together until pale and fluffy. Gradually incorporate the eggs, beating well as you go. Add in half the flour, folding it in gently with a metal spoon. Then fold in the rest. Divide half the mixture between the two tins and bake in a pre-heated oven at 375°F (190°C) for about 20 minutes until well risen. When cool, sandwich the two halves together with the jam or preserve and dust the top with sieved icing or confectioner's sugar. Place on an elegant cake stand.

Trifle

Another British tea-time favourite. The Italians seemed to have liked the idea too – their version is called Zuppa Inglese and usually has a chocolate custard layer. Trifle looks best in a glass bowl so that the different layers can be seen from the sides.

Fill the bottom of a large bowl with jam swiss roll or sponge cake spread with raspberry jam and broken into pieces. Cover this with fresh or frozen raspberries and a generous glass of sherry. Mix well and allow all the ingredients to soak together. Make a thick custard (*see* page 47) and allow it to cool. Pour a layer of custard over the sponge cake and raspberries. Whip up sufficient double (heavy) cream to make a generous layer on top. Decorate with flaked almonds and chill before serving.

John Shirley-Fox (1860-1939) *The White Tablecloth*

Mayonnaise

This sauce has ancient origins and is made by a magical process whereby quite ordinary ingredients are suddenly transformed into a new shining, golden form. There was a time when the sauce was always made by hand and some people find it rather soothing to continue with this old method, slowly adding the oil to the egg yolks drop by drop. Luckily, there is an easy way to produce a mayonnaise which is very nearly as good as the original.

Place 2 whole eggs in the food processor together with a crushed clove of garlic, a teaspoon of mustard powder and salt and ground black pepper. Then, with the motor running, pour in 10 fl oz (1¹/₄ cups) of groundnut or a light olive oil in a steady stream. Pour in a little white wine vinegar, tasting as you go. Once you have made mayonnaise you have the basis of several other sauces, *aïoli*, which has a great deal of garlic added to it and is served as a vegetable dip or with fish: *tartare*, which is simply a basic mayonnaise finished with some chopped gherkin (pickle) and chopped capers and parsley and is ideal with grilled or fried fish, and *rouille* which contains garlic, lemon juice instead of vinegar, tomato purée and cayenne pepper, the amount depending on how much 'kick' you require. This is traditionally spread on croûtons, sprinkled with grated Gruyère cheese and served with the classic *bouillabaisse* and fish soups of Marseille.

Edgar Hunt (1876-1955) *Feeding Time*, 1928

44

Pipérade

The people in the picture have come to the end of a pleasant lunch and are now taking coffee and liqueurs. The lady probably started her meal with something like a pipérade, almost a meal in itself, followed by a light second course and little else. This concoction of eggs and peppers originated in the Basque region but is known the length and breadth of France and beyond. Made with 4 eggs it would be an ample first course for 2 people.

Start by frying a finely chopped onion in olive oil till transparent. Add 6 de-seeded green peppers cut into large strips. Cook for 15 minutes then add 2 lb (1 kg) ripe tomatoes, skinned and roughly chopped, a little crushed garlic, a pinch of dried basil and salt and pepper. When the tomatoes are cooked to a pulp add the well beaten eggs and stir into the mixture, cooking it until it begins to look like something halfway between scrambled eggs and a lightly cooked omelette. Turn the *pipérade* out onto a hot serving dish and serve with a slice of grilled ham or on its own with a few croûtons.

Pierre Auguste Renoir (1841-1919) *The Lunch*

45

Farmhouse Fruit Cake

This is an everyday kind of cake, useful for packed lunches or for taking on a picnic. It can be made with sultanas or raisins or a mixture of the two and has long been a family favourite. Despite introductions from elsewhere, the sun-dried fruits produced around Izmir, in Turkey, have long been among the very best and still are. Avoid fruit which has a glossy finish as it has probably been coated in mineral oil.

Butter and line a large cake tin. Soak 8 oz (1½ cups) raisins and sultanas for at least an hour in lukewarm water to plump them up. Beat 8 oz (1 cup) unsalted butter until smooth and creamy. Add 8 oz (1 cup) sugar, 2 eggs and 3 egg yolks and mix well. Drain the fruit thoroughly and mix it into 1 lb 2 oz (4½ cups) sifted flour with a good pinch of cinnamon. Mix the egg mixture in then fold in a few tablespoons of rum and the stiffly beaten whites of the 3 eggs. Pour into the cake tin, which should not be quite full, and bake in a pre-heated oven at 350°F (180°C) for 1½ to 2 hours.

James Jacques Joseph Tissot (1836-1902) *The Picnic*

46

Eugène Boudin (1824-1898) *Animals in a Pond*

Custard Sauce

Although ready-made versions are available they are usually made from inferior ingredients and bear practically no resemblance to the real thing. It is well worth taking the trouble to make this sauce for a special occasion to serve with a home-made classic desserts such as apple pie, steamed fruit or jam puddings and to add to trifles.

Bring 10 fl oz (1 cup) of cream up to boiling point but do not actually boil. Thoroughly blend 3 egg yolks, a teaspoon of cornflour (cornstarch), a tablespoon of castor sugar and a few drops of real vanilla essence together in a small basin. Pour the hot cream on top, stirring all the while, then return to the saucepan. Heat very gently, still stirring until the sauce has thickened. It can be served either hot or chilled to complement the rest of the dessert.

Imperial/Metric Conversion

Weights

2 oz	50 g
2½ oz	60 g
3 oz	75 g
4 oz	110 g
4½ oz	125 g
5 oz	150 g
6 oz	175 g
7 oz	200 g
8 oz	225 g
9 oz	250 g
10 oz	275 g
12 oz	350 g
1 lb	450 g
1½ lb	700 g
2 lb	900 g
3 lb	1.3 kg

Volume

5 fl oz (¼ pt)	150 ml
10 fl oz (½ pt)	275 ml
15 fl oz (¾ pt)	425 ml
1 pint	570 ml
1¼ pints	725 ml
1¾ pints	1 litre
2 pints	1.2 litres
2½ pints	1.5 litres
4 pints	2.25 litres

Index

Walter Hunt (1861-1941) *A Devonshire Farm Yard*